ICE ROAD TRUCKER

BY NICK GORDON

BELLWETHER MEDIA · MINNEAPOLIS, MN

Are you ready to take it to the extreme?
Torque books thrust you into the action-packed world
of sports, vehicles, mystery, and adventure. These books
may include dirt, smoke, fire, and dangerous stunts.
WARNING: read at your own risk.

Library of Congress Cataloging-in-Publication Data

Gordon, Nick.
 Ice road trucker / by Nick Gordon.
    pages cm. -- (Torque : dangerous jobs)
 Includes bibliographical references and index.
 Summary: "Engaging images accompany information about ice road truckers. The combination of
high-interest subject matter and light text is intended for students in grades 3 through 7"--Provided
by publisher.
 ISBN 978-1-60014-895-8 (hbk : alk. paper)
 1. Truck drivers--Juvenile literature. 2. Trucking--Juvenile literature. 3. Trucking--Arctic regions--
Juvenile literature. 4. Ice crossings--Juvenile literature. I. Title.
 HD8039.M795G67 2013
 388.3'4409113--dc23
                                        2012041222

This edition first published in 2013 by Bellwether Media, Inc.

Printed in the United States of America, North Mankato, MN.

TABLE OF CONTENTS

CHAPTER 1

THIN ICE

An 18-wheeler rumbles over a frozen lake in northern Canada. Gusts of wind kick up snow and make it hard to see. The truck's big tires slip and slide. The driver keeps the truck moving. If he stops, the truck might fall through the ice!

A strong gust hits the side of the truck. The **trailer** skids to one side. The driver acts fast. He turns the steering wheel and straightens out the truck. He does not stop driving. The ice will crack if he slows down. It is just another day of work as an ice road trucker.

Cashing In

Ice road truckers can make a lot of money. Each trip they make is called a run. On average, a trucker receives about $2,000 per run. In a few months, they can earn more than $120,000.

CHAPTER 2

ICE ROAD TRUCKERS

8

Ice road truckers haul **freight** across some of the most dangerous roads in the world. They drive over frozen lakes and ice-covered stretches. Some travel up steep hills and mountains. Roads are narrow and have many sharp turns. One mistake can result in disaster!

Ice road truckers can work only a few months of the year. They carry supplies to Alaska, Canada, and other northern regions during the coldest part of winter. That is when the ice on lakes is thick enough to support their trucks and trailers.

Truck **maintenance** is the key to safety for ice road truckers. They must keep their trucks in top condition. They give the trucks **anti-lock brakes**. These brakes prevent the tires from skidding.

Keep It Moving

Ice road truckers usually drive about 15 miles (24 kilometers) per hour on ice. Faster speeds can make waves in the water beneath the ice. Slower speeds can cause the ice to crack.

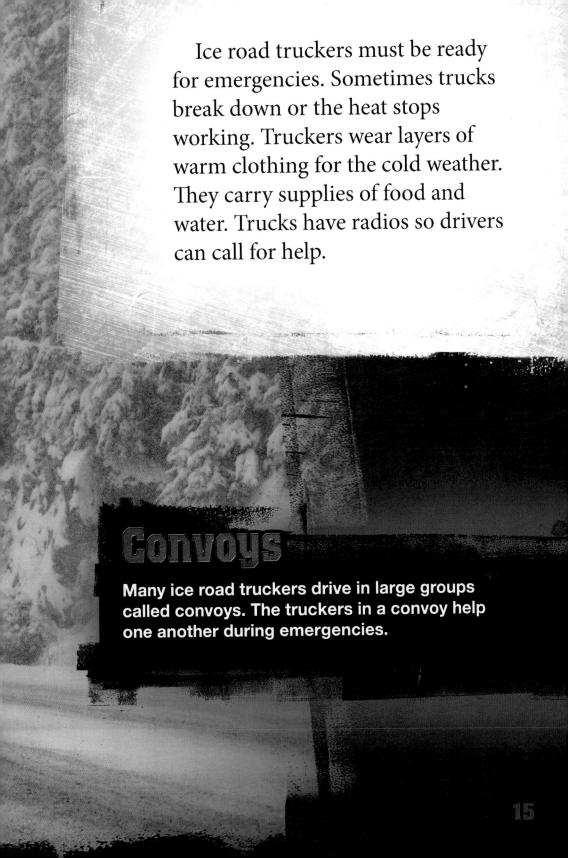

Ice road truckers must be ready for emergencies. Sometimes trucks break down or the heat stops working. Truckers wear layers of warm clothing for the cold weather. They carry supplies of food and water. Trucks have radios so drivers can call for help.

Convoys

Many ice road truckers drive in large groups called convoys. The truckers in a convoy help one another during emergencies.

CHAPTER 3

DANGER!

Ice road trucking is filled with dangers. Trucks can crash down steep mountains or cliffs. Roads can fall apart beneath a truck's tires. Trucks that break down can fall through the ice. Anyone caught inside a truck during such an accident is in great danger.

Whiteout

The weather is another threat to ice road truckers. They are exposed to bitter cold and strong winds. They can get **frostbite** in minutes. **Hypothermia** is an even bigger danger. Truckers **stranded** outside or in freezing water can lose body heat fast. Their organs eventually shut down.

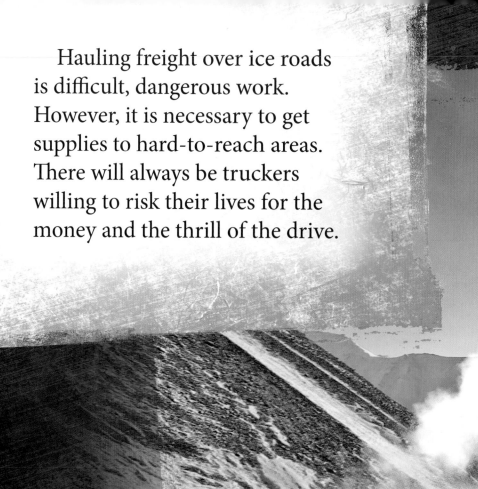

Hauling freight over ice roads is difficult, dangerous work. However, it is necessary to get supplies to hard-to-reach areas. There will always be truckers willing to risk their lives for the money and the thrill of the drive.

Tragedy on the Job

In 2007, ice road trucker Dale Harris was killed on Alaska's Dalton Highway. Another truck's tires had lost their grip during a run. Harris died when the truck's trailer spun around and slammed into him.

Glossary

anti-lock brakes—a braking system that uses bursts of braking pressure to reduce the risk of locking; locked brakes stop a vehicle's wheels from turning and cause it to skid.

freight—goods carried by truck, train, ship, or aircraft

frostbite—a condition in which body tissues are damaged by extreme cold

hypothermia—a condition in which the body loses heat faster than it can produce it; hypothermia causes body systems to shut down.

maintenance—the practice of keeping something in good working condition

stranded—left in a place with no way to get out

trailer—the part of a truck that holds the freight

To Learn More

AT THE LIBRARY

Gustaitis, Joseph Alan. *Arctic Trucker*. New York, N.Y.: Marshall Cavendish Benchmark, 2011.

Ransom, Candice F. *Big Rigs*. Minneapolis, Minn.: Lerner Publications, 2011.

Reeves, Diane Lindsey. *Scary Jobs*. New York, N.Y.: Ferguson, 2009.

ON THE WEB

Learning more about ice road truckers is as easy as 1, 2, 3.

1. Go to www.factsurfer.com.

2. Enter "ice road truckers" into the search box.

3. Click the "Surf" button and you will see a list of related Web sites.

With factsurfer.com, finding more information is just a click away.

Index